HANDBOOK OF HUMAN FORMATION: A RESOURCE FOR THE CULTIVATION OF CHARACTER

Essential Foundations of the Art & Science of Human Formation for University, College, and Seminary Staff

Cameron M. Thompson, MA

Published by Acropolis Scholars, LLC
St. Paul, Minnesota.

ISBN: 978-0692302774

Preface

Those of us placed in a position of authority and leadership in service of others have, by the nature of our position, the responsibility to help them become men and women of virtue and integrity, capable of cultivating that virtue and integrity in others – in a word, we are responsible for their Human Formation. This is a responsibility that we cannot afford to ignore. These individuals have been entrusted to our guidance by Providence, to cooperate in helping each one become all that he or she is meant to be in the sight of God. This is all the more so true for those with the responsibility for the Human Formation of young people in colleges, universities, seminaries, or schools. These young people are in the most formative stage in their life outside of infancy. The reality of the matter is that your actions and activities are already having an impact on their Human Formation, consciously or unconsciously, for good or for ill. By recognizing this fact and taking the appropriate steps, you can fulfill your responsibility to help each one manifest in himself or herself as far as possible the human perfection shining forth in the Incarnate Son of God.

The term 'Human Formation' first entered official usage in 1992 in St. John Paul II's post-synodal apostolic exhortation, *Pastores Dabo Vobis*, on the formation of priests. The term refers to the basic and essential formation of the human person as person, aimed at bringing that individual into full Affective Maturity. Human Formation consists in large part in the formation of character undertaken through a holistic understanding of the human person and the nature of human flourishing. Unlike most other approaches to character formation, however, rather than seeking to fulfill a merely utilitarian end (e.g. social competence, career success), Human Formation has as its aim nothing less than that the individual human person should manifest in him or herself as far as possible the "human perfection which shines forth in the Incarnate Son of God."

Since being brought into official usage in 1992, the term 'Human Formation' has been bandied about in various circles, with no clear and coherent sense of what it really means or how it works. This present work provides an introduction to the art and science of Human

Formation, along with some practical principles for putting it into practice.

What follows herein is a brief overview of a systematic approach to Human Formation, and should serve as a basic but necessary foundation for those seeking a comprehensive and systematic treatment of the art and science of Human Formation. This present work, and other forthcoming related works are the fruit of extensive research and experience working in the field of Human Formation and Character Development, from its foundations in philosophical theory to the scientific principles of psychology engaged in its practical implementation. This approach and method of Human Formation is built on the moral tradition of the Church, centered on a sound Thomistic Anthropology, and supported by the best of contemporary psychological research.

Who this Book is For

This book is for those who are responsible in some way for the Human Formation, moral development, or leadership training of others. This responsibility might be explicit or implicit, but if you have some sort of responsibility for others, be assured, the duty of having in mind the Human Formation and character development of those under your charge falls, even if only in part, on your shoulders.

This particular work is written for the benefit of those individuals who intend to implement in some way a concrete program of Human Formation, especially those who intend to do so in their capacity as Residence Directors, RA's, Residence Life Staff, Seminary Formation Faculty, or Program Coordinators. Naturally, it will also benefit many others who have in some way or other the responsibility for the formation of young men and women.

Table of Contents

Part I: Definition and Scope of Human Formation

The Task of Human Formation

Human Formation is the *necessary foundation* for the other three pillars of Christian Formation (Spiritual, Intellectual, and Pastoral/Apostolic). It should be noted that Human Formation is entirely distinct from what is called "human development." 'Human Development' refers to the natural, more or less passive progression of stages within the human lifecycle, while 'Human Formation' refers to the intentional cultivation and formation of character of the whole Human Person to his or her natural perfection.

Human Formation has as its aim nothing less than to develop the character of the individual human person that he or she manifest in him or herself as far as possible, the "human perfection which shines forth in the Incarnate Son of God."[1]

To elaborate, Human Formation aims at perfecting the natural human qualities of the

---

[1] *Pastores Dabo Vobis*, 43.

person as the "raw material" for sanctity. It is the process of attaining the highest and best of one's human nature and the fulfillment of that human nature as it is instantiated in this or that particular person.

An Extensive Undertaking

This work of ever-perfecting the natural human qualities of the person is a life-long undertaking, begun *even while in the womb*,[2] and continuing unto death; **informed and brought to completion by, but essentially distinct from, the Divine Life of Grace**. This formation of personal character is all-encompassing, in that everything we do as persons has an effect on our character in some way or another, and so there is nothing in the natural life of the person that isn't in some way related to Human Formation. In fact, we are continuously being formed by our habitual actions, environment, relationships, and "formative micro-

---

[2] New studies are showing that various personality characteristics, psychological dispositions, and neurological patterns already are taking shape in the life of the child *in utero* – that not only genetic determinates, but the actions and even psycho-physiological state of the mother affect the pre-natal development of the child.

practices"[3] every day, for good or for ill. What we need to do is become intentional about whether we are allowing ourselves to become malformed by these thoughts and habits, or forming ourselves (and one another) into the "fullness of the stature of Jesus Christ."[4]

Those responsible for the formation of others must be aware, however, that various aspects of contemporary society often put young men and women at a disadvantage vis-à-vis Affective Maturity and healthy Psycho-Sexual Identity. That is, young men and women are not coming in as "blank slates" ready for further formation, but are often in deep need of healing the malformation resultant from personal history/upbringing; Human Formation must be remedial as well as positively-formative.

---

[3] For more on formative micro-practices and the pedagogy of desire, see James K.A. Smith's work in *Desiring the Kingdom* and *Imagining the Kingdom*. Grand Rapids, MI: Baker Academic, 2009.

[4] Ephesians 4:13

Relation of Human Formation to the other Pillars of Christian Formation

Intellectual Formation: Human Formation disciplines and purifies the intellect through virtue and humility, and is in turn enlightened and cultured by Intellectual Formation. "The truth springs up in the same soil as the good: their roots communicate. Broken from their common root [...] one or the other suffers; the soul grows anemic or the mind wilts."[5]

Pastoral/Apostolic Formation: Human Formation imparts necessary experience, wisdom, and virtue to the one engaged in apostolic work, and in turn Pastoral Formation reveals further areas for growth in Human Formation, and the encounter with the reality of Pastoral situations shapes the character of the apostle.[6]

---

[5] A. Sertillanges, *The Intellectual Life*. Translated by Mary Ryan. Westminster, MD: Newman Press, 1948, p. 23.

[6] Christ spent 30 years in Human Formation before beginning public pastoral work. The apostles learned Christ first (through his humanity) before being sent out, and even then they returned for further Human Formation before being sent out again.

Spiritual Formation: Human Formation disciplines and grounds Spirituality in authenticity, and prepares the offering of one's humanity & personality to God in prayer. Spiritual Formation cooperates with Human Formation to allow grace to heal the heart. *Grace builds on and perfects Nature.*[7]

Distinct Domains of Spiritual Formation and Human Formation

Spiritual Formation deals with the life of grace and the supernatural, Human Formation deals with *natural human qualities of the person* (psychology, virtue, personality, habits, etc.) There is a grave danger in thinking that one can just perform certain spiritual devotions and that will be enough for attaining virtue. On the contrary, if one is not fully grounded in an authentic humanity and

---

[7] Human Formation is often downplayed or, at best, misunderstood. We see the full perfection of Christ shine through His **humanity.** Christ spent 30 years consisting simply of family life during which he did little to reveal His Divinity; He lived a very ordinary, but perfect, human life. Before any pastoral work, or spiritual teaching, before miracles, He spent 30 years of intensive living-out of humanity. His life consisted of labor, family life, obedience to (even fallible) human authority.

perfecting natural qualities by means proper to the natural realm, he or she will develop a warped and unhealthy spirituality as well as a stunted and twisted human nature. We should no sooner presume for God to miraculously make men into learned scholars without studying, eloquent orators without practice, or skilled rugby players without training, than for them to be perfected in virtue and skill and psychologically sound & mature, without work and practice by natural means.

The Goal of Human Formation

The *telos* of Human Formation is to form a "Man of Communion."[8] "The Man of Communion is capable of making a gift of himself and of receiving the gift of others. This, in fact, requires the full possession of oneself."[9] In other words, the Man or Woman of Communion manifests (1) full self-possession, (2) the capacity for the sincere and authentic gift of self to others, and (3) the capacity

---

[8] This is the term used by the foundational text in the *Program of Priestly Formation*; it is in the masculine form since it is fundamentally Christological in its orientation, but applies equally to men and women.

[9] *Program for Priestly Formation (PPF)*, 76.

to receive the self-gift of others. The 'communion' referred to in the term 'Man of Communion' is brought about through knowledge and love;[10] this must be a proper knowledge of and rightly ordered love for self, others, and God. Thus the communion which characterizes the Man or Woman of Communion is threefold: union of integrity with self, interpersonal union with others in healthy and mature relationships, and ultimately, an ever-growing union with God. Christ, as the *perfectus homo*, is the exemplary Man of Communion.

At the core of his or her being, the human person is made for communion, and so it is that the Man or Woman of Communion is one who is in a significant degree oriented toward the perfection of his or her human nature – in other words, becoming a well-formed and perfect human person.

So how does one recognize a Man or Woman of Communion? The *PPF* articulates the following key characteristic markers: the person who is in

---

[10] See Aquinas, *Summa Theologiae, Ia-IIae, q.28, a.1.*

full possession of himself, is generous and approachable, and whose relational capacities are real and deep.[11]

The Matter of Human Formation

The matter of Human Formation, the subject to be formed, is nothing less than the human person in his or her entirety. Under the aspect of being the material object of Human Formation, the direct aims of Human Formation qua the person-being-formed can nevertheless be laid out in a distinct systematic taxonomy: **Formation of the Heart**, **Cultivation of Virtue**, and **Acquisition of Practical Skills**.

The Process of Human Formation

Human Formation is not one static thing, but an ongoing process of development and becoming. Rooted in the foundation of a healthy *Self-Identity*, Human Formation becomes a dynamic three-fold process of a *Self-Knowledge* that leads to *Self-Acceptance* which flows out in *Self-Gift*. This process of formation plays out in the **Formation of the Heart**, which extends in the

[11] *PPF*, 76

Cultivation of Virtue, through the **Acquisition of Practical Skills**.

Self-Identity, the Foundation of Self-Knowledge

Becoming a Man or Woman of Communion begins with being at one with oneself. This requires a proper understanding of one's self-identity. Without a proper and healthy **Self-Identity**, the individual cannot authentically become a Man of Communion in relation to others and to God; because the individual is not in full possession of himself (he doesn't even know who he is).

Self-Identity starts with the proper anthropological understanding of human nature and from that core, a healthy personal self-identity can be formed. A proper **anthropological self-identity** is an essential prerequisite for a healthy and accurate **personal self-identity**.

Anthropological Self-Identity, what it means to be a human person, body & soul, made in the image and likeness of God, answers the question, *"What am I?"* It must both take into account the various fields of scientific knowledge about man and also be rooted in a real and personal encounter and union with "Christ, the final Adam [who] reveals man to man himself."[12]

Personal Self-Identity is the personal appropriation of how one's anthropological self-identity is integrated within the context of the individual's life experiences. It answers the question, *"Who am I?"* A healthy and accurate personal self-identity requires a substantial degree of **Existential Integrity** – the harmonious integrity of the immanent and transcendent dimensions of the self. These two dimensions of personal self-identity (i.e. immanence and transcendence) are interdependent co-principles of the experience of the self. When isolated from one another, each leads to a deformed experience of the self and a structurally unsound personal self-identity. Such an isolation or dichotomy causes the individual to suffer an unhealthy psychological paradigm, which in time leads to existential despair and a double-life in vain attempts at creating a unified self-identity.

---

[12] *Gaudium et Spes*, 22.

On the other hand, the one whose personal self-identity is marked by Existential Integrity is the one who fully embodies the self-identity of a person in communion with other persons, and alone is free to be who he or she is in God's design. Such a person has a deep connection to the real world, and at the same time realizes the call to union with the infinite God even in the here and now, indeed, specifically in and through the here and now, as *Homo Viator – Man the Wayfarer*.

Without the proper foundation of a Personal Self-Identity marked by Existential Integrity, the whole work of Human Formation would be "like a house built on sand"[13] for it would be fragmented at its very core.

Self-Knowledge

Self-Identity is distinct from, but prerequisite for Self-Knowledge – knowing things about oneself. Personal Self-Identity is the individual and personal appropriation of a proper understanding of what it means to be a human person, a self in communion with other selves, within the context

---

[13] Cf. Matthew 7:26-27

of one's own individual experiences. Self-Knowledge is the awareness of one's own habits, personality, experiences, strengths, weaknesses, etc. Self-Knowledge, framed within the context of Self-Identity, is thus the awareness of one's personal qualities and how they affect his or her relationship with others, with God, and with himself or herself. Just as Anthropological and Personal Self-Identity answer the questions, *"What am I?"* and *"Who am I?"* Self-Knowledge, as such, answers the question, *"How am I?"* (i.e. *"What kind of person am I?"*).

Self-Acceptance

A proper foundation in a healthy self-identity allows **Self-Acceptance** to flow from **Self-Knowledge** in the humble acknowledgement of one's personal qualities. Self-Knowledge & Self-Acceptance cooperate to manifest in **personal integrity**, which is the seamless continuity of one's Personal Self-Identity and one's Self-Presentation (how the individual presents himself or herself to others). **Personal Integrity** requires maintaining the intimate connection and continuity of all one's experiences and attitudes in everyday circumstances in a raw and open honesty with God.

Self-Gift

Existential Integrity in one's **Self-Identity** flows through **Personal Integrity** into **Self-Gift**. Self-Gift is expressed and realized through virtue, both personal and relational. Every encounter with another person is an opportunity for Self-Gift.

Becoming a Man or Woman of Communion

This is in essence, what it means to be a Man or Woman of Communion: Being at one with yourself, knowing who you are and your place in this world as a personal self in communion with other personal selves,[14] knowing and accepting your personal qualities and experiences,[15] and giving yourself to God and neighbor through the perfection of your human nature in the development of virtue and sincere, charitable encounters with others.[16]

---

[14] i.e. Self-Identity

[15] i.e. Self-Knowledge & Self-Acceptance

[16] i.e. Self-Gift

The entirety of this dynamic unfolding of **Self-Identity** and **Self-Knowledge,** leading to **Self-Acceptance,** and flowing out in **Self-Gift,** plays out first and foremost in the Formation of the Heart.

Formation of the Heart

"[Christ, the perfect man] worked with human hands, thought with a human mind, acted by human choice, and loved with a human heart"[17]

Human Formation finds its origin and end in the Formation of the Heart – the center of personhood – for all virtues, traits, and skills follow from Formation of the Heart, as action follows being.[18] Virtue is only perfect insofar as it flows from a healthy Self-Identity and in turn further shapes that identity. Without this foundation in the Formation of the Heart, all other aspects of Human Formation will crumble and fall. Of all things in Human Formation, this is truly fundamental.[19]

A properly formed heart is what makes the Man or Woman of Communion. The Heart is the basic capacity of the person to Love, and love is what brings about communion between persons. To love another person means to seek communion

---

[17] *GS*, 22.

[18] Application of the classic Thomistic-Aristotelian maxim, *agere sequitur esse*.

[19] *Pastores Dabo Vobis*, 43.

with the beloved and will good for the beloved; to love non-persons is to seek union with those things as useful or good for one's self. Formation of the Heart, then, at its core has to do with healing, ordering, and perfecting the subject's capacity for love. Thus, becoming a Man or Woman of Communion is the effect of the Formation of the Heart, just as union is an effect of love. This love is not an unemotional act of "dry will" but necessarily involves the affective and emotional capacities of the human person in the fullness of man's dignity and splendor.[20]

"Man cannot live without love. He remains a thing that is incomprehensible to himself, […] if he does not experience it and make it his own, if he does not participate intimately in it."[21]

The Cultivation of Virtue

Love, the *virtus unitiva*, is the basic principle and power at the core of man's being that puts in motion all his other passions and actions. This basic power of love is formed, developed, and

---

[20] See *Summa Theologiae, Ia-IIae,* q.26, a.1 & 2.

[21] *Redemptor Hominis,* 10.

directed through the virtues which shape and perfect his powers and faculties to love in an ordered, rather than disordered, way, and this through the Practical Skills which hone his ability to love and act in the best possible manner.

The moral virtues deal with the perfection of the natural powers of man, and so are properly the domain of Human Formation, rather than Spiritual Formation (which deals with the life of Grace, the Supernatural Virtues of Faith, Hope, Charity, and the Gifts of the Spirit). Human Formation of the moral virtues is the necessary and prerequisite foundation for the supernatural virtues and gifts.[22] Another point worth mentioning is that the natural moral virtues are not a disconnected array of various qualities, but are intimately inter-related in a systematic hierarchy and taxonomy,[23] the understanding of which is of vital importance for anyone responsible for the moral development and formation of others.

---

[22] See *Summa Theologiae Ia-IIae, q.68, a.8, ad 2.*

[23] A concise chart and commentary on this taxonomy can be found below in **Part V. A Guide to the Virtues.**

The power of example is one of the single most important factors in determining what course of action a man or woman will take in a new or unfamiliar situation.[24] This means that one must have foresight and take care regarding what examples one puts before his or her eyes, by way of movies, books, companions, etc. Imagination and Memory are more powerful than Cognition; the imprint of examples and past experiences runs deeper and on a more primal level than conscious reason so long as one remains unaware of it. This is why, in order to cultivate virtue, it is vital to develop the habit of awareness of the movement of one's own thoughts, emotions, and desires.[25]

The power of example and imaginative memory notwithstanding, it is also important to cultivate virtue on the level of conscious reason by interiorizing maxims of wisdom and the law which provide general principles of right action. Nevertheless, it should always be remembered that

---

[24] Studies have shown that in new situations, we're more likely to imitate those we've previously observed under similar circumstances (often following the example of parents/mentors and film or television characters).

[25] This will be further developed in **Part II** & **Part IV**.

the power of example is stronger than the power of precept.

The actual Cultivation of Virtue requires two things: **(1) Mimetic Knowledge**: an example of virtuous action for the individual to imitate[26], and **(2) Opportunity**: a situation which challenges and demands a virtuous action to achieve a desired outcome. Without the first, the individual will not know how to act rightly; without the second, his or her knowledge is of no avail, since there is no opportunity for virtue to be put into practice, and so actually cultivated.

*The sole means of acquiring the **habitus**[27] of virtue are consistent and repeated individual intentional acts*

---

[26] The example can come through different media (personal experience, or the vicarious experience of an exemplar obtained through stories or relationships, etc.). Easier circumstances demand lesser, or more abstract (or imaginatively synthesized) examples, tougher circumstances demand more concrete and real exemplars. Virtue comes more readily through *mimesis* than through formal instruction.

[27] A 'habitus' is a deeply abiding quality of character that disposes the person toward some kind of action/feeling or another, and can be either a strength (i.e. virtue) or weakness (i.e. vice). A habitus involves all three primary faculties of the human person: Reason, Will, and Emotion/Sensation, and so cannot be acquired or changed by sheer force of will, nor by mere instruction, but only by progressive alteration of routine

of virtue. These individual acts of virtue ordinarily occur in the framework of daily activity, and can be both manifested in and formed by the **Practical Skills**. Virtue must be built by degrees, starting with lesser challenges, and ascending to the higher through mastery of the lower. One truly has acquired the habitus of virtue when he or she takes pleasure in the particular act of virtue as second-nature to his very personhood.

---

practices and habits.

Acquisition of Practical Skills

*"Finally, brethren, whatever is true, whatever is
honorable, whatever is just, whatever is pure, whatever
is lovely, whatever is gracious, if there is any excellence,
if there is anything worthy of praise, think about these
things. What you have learned and received and heard
and seen in me, do; and the God of peace will be with
you."*[28]

These Practical Skills facilitate the Gift of Self in
the real, concrete circumstances of everyday life,
and are in themselves minor perfections of the
correlative virtues. There are a number of central
and supporting skills that facilitate and even make
possible the interpersonal communion which is the
desire of every human heart. These skills can, in
an inchoate form, be learned primarily from
instruction, but must still be put into practice for
them to become in any sense a real skill. Like the
virtues, these Practical Skills have their own
proper hierarchy and taxonomy, being divided
first into **Personal Skills** and **Social Skills**. The
Personal Skills in turn are divided into the
domains of *Religious Practices, Physical Self-Care,*

---

[28] Philippians 4:8

and *Psychological Self-Care*; the **Social Skills** are divided into the domains of *Relationship*, *Deportment*, and *Professional Skills*. A detailed guide to these skills is provided in **Part VI** of this book.

The Social Skills, and in an ancillary way, the Personal Skills, essentially amount to being a Courteous Lady or Gentleman, competent in one's role as a social being. Courtesy is an act of dying to self and of giving one's self to others; thus courtesy is the beginning of Charity. This courtesy is the first step and outward demeanor of the authentic Man or Woman of Communion, and does not mean being a foppish or preening etiquette snob, but rather being thoughtful, considerate, and polite.[29]

Summary of the Process of Human Formation

The Formation of the Heart – Self-Identity, Self-Knowledge, Self-Acceptance, and Self-Gift – is manifested in Personal Integrity and in the authentic Cultivation of Virtue. Virtues, as deeply

---

[29] Cf. Archbishop Timothy Dolan, in *Priests for the Third Millenium*. Huntington, IN: Our Sunday Visitor, 2000. p. 90.

abiding qualities of character, cannot be seen in themselves, but only becomes manifest in concrete acts, most especially the Practical Skills, both Personal and Social. This process in turn works reflexively: The Practical Skills facilitate the Cultivation of Virtue, which in turn further develops and deepens the Formation of the Heart.

Affective Maturity

A proper understanding of Affective Maturity requires an understanding and appreciation of the centrality of love in human existence, in other words, an appreciation of the central role of love as the principle that motivates all the other passions and actions of a person. In order to understand Affective Maturity, one must first understand that the human person is first of all a loving being, rather than a Cartesian *res cogitans*. This means that Affective Maturity requires the healthy formation and maturation of this capacity to love. It should be noted, that although Affective Maturity entails the virtuous ordering of the emotions and desires ("affections"), it is not merely emotional maturity. Affective Maturity refers to the maturity of the whole *affectus* – the appetites and desires, **including the "rational appetite" (the will)**. That is to say, it refers to the mature and virtuously ordered heart – the core of personhood, the basic and most fundamental disposition of the human person.

As such, Affective Maturity is the "adjectival quality" of the Man or Woman of Communion, and so is the developmental way to talk about the level of Human Formation proper to any stage in life. Forming the "Man of Communion" is the end-goal of Human Formation, and it is the Formation of the Heart, the Virtues, and the Practical Skills that makes the individual more perfectly a Man or Woman of Communion by increasing Affective Maturity.

Practically speaking, the formation of Affective Maturity requires the habit of presence and awareness, both of one's own interior emotions and desires, those of others, and awareness of one's environment.

Incommunicable Mystery of the Self

Now, it is not enough to simply become a generic cookie-cutter "Man of Communion" – indeed, given the unrepeatable subjectivity of the individual human person, it would be a great failure of Human Formation to produce such a result. No, Human Formation has only really "worked" if "being a man of communion" manifests in this particular man or woman becoming more fully and properly a Personal Self, one who is more fully himself or herself as God intends him or her to be, with all of his or her unique and unrepeatable characteristics and attributes – not in their raw and disordered state, but in their dynamically virtuous and integrated perfection. All Human Formation must be brought down to the concrete level of the individual person and his or her individual personality and character. Each individual human person, properly formed as a Man or Woman of Communion, is an unrepeatable work of art designed by God and executed by the cooperation between God, the individual, and those responsible for his or her Human Formation. This cannot come about by merely putting on the mask of a generic "Man of Communion." It needs to grow out of becoming, in radically genuine authenticity, this particular Man or Woman of Communion, virtuous and free.

Part II: Basic Principles for a Program of Human Formation

The practical implementation of a Human Formation program is a complex affair. The skills, actions, relationships, and environment relate to the actual development of virtue and identity in a very complex way; indeed, all personal acts themselves relate to an array of different virtues and skills at play. One needs to look at Human Formation in two ways: the Ontological perspective (the aim and scope of Human Formation covered in Part I), and the Programmatic perspective (how Human Formation actually happens). Part II will look at Human Formation from the Programmatic perspective.

Human Formation happens through **Formative Experiences**, which take place within **Three Core Arenas** of the everyday life of the individual, and are brought about by way of specific, concrete, intentional means which we will call the "**Tools of Human Formation**."

Caveat: A Person, not a Product

Despite the reality that Human Formation is a process that can and must be done with intentionality and in a programmatic way, those responsible for Human Formation program need to keep in mind the unique exigencies of each Individual Person. The human person cannot be treated as a mere product on an assembly line, with quality checks to pass or imperfections to be corrected; the person must always be approached as a real Self-In-Communion, that is, be approached with the aim of helping him or her become ever more "perfect as your heavenly Father is perfect."[30]

The difference between these two approaches, spoken or unspoken, explicit or subtle, is very clearly and impactfully communicated through the pedagogical environment and the attitude of those responsible for Human Formation. The work of Human Formation can only be accomplished correctly and effectively if it is flowing from a proper orientation to the dignity of the individual

---

[30] Matthew 5:48

human person. Those responsible for Human Formation must put on the Heart of Christ. Only then can the men and women under their charge become Men and Women of Communion in the image and likeness of Christ the Perfect Man.

Foundational Elements

There are prerequisites for any organization to have in order before effective Human Formation can occur – these are necessary, but not sufficient, conditions that set up a favorable environment for Human Formation to take place. Those responsible for Human Formation ought to take stock of these **10 Foundational Elements** before embarking on the endeavor of implementing a Human Formation program.

1. **Actually Having an Intentional Human Formation Program:** The reality of the matter is that formation of some sort, for better or worse, is already taking place regardless of whether we are being intentional about it or not. In order to avoid malformation, one needs to pay explicit attention to what Formative Experiences are taking place for a person

within the Three Core Arenas of their life, and what effect it is having. Such an intentional program needs to be coherent and systematic if it is to have the greatest positive effect. Character development or change is far more effective when it is addressed on multiple fronts, and so it is important that such a program be multidimensional, as will be developed in what follows.

2. **Culture of Excellence**: Those responsible for Human Formation need to foster a culture of excellence in their organization. Strive for the best; demand the best of human nature, since the aim of Human Formation is to develop those very natural qualities of the person as the raw material for sanctity, and sets it sight on nothing less than "the human perfection which shines forth in the Incarnate Son of God."[31] No virtue can grow in the bitter soil of cynicism and pusillanimity.[32]

---

[31] Cf. *Pastores Dabo Vobis*.

[32] Cf. *Rule of St. Benedict*, 41: "manage and adapt everything that souls may be saved, and that what the brethren do, they

3. **Exemplary Faculty & Staff**: Those responsible for Human Formation need to be well formed themselves to some degree. A mal-formed leadership breeds cynicism, contempt, and superficiality. The fact is that those in authority are role models either way, for good or for ill, and cannot rest on their laurels. They need to be open to continually growing in their own Human Formation.

4. **Trust**: This is a skill that often has yet to be learned by many people. Trust can be defined as the confident belief that the other has your best interest at heart, **and is competent to help you achieve it**. This is built by vulnerability, love, and demonstrated loyalty. A lack of trust is the one thing that can erode the whole program of Human Formation.

5. **Community Life**: The human person is a social being, made for community. No virtue can be developed in man without a community in which those virtues can be

---

may do without having a reasonable cause to murmur."

lived out. Some sense of belonging to a real, concrete, tangible community must be present for a Human Formation program to be effective.

6. **Virtuous Friendships**: True & healthy friendships are essential in the acquisition of Affective Maturity. This provides the imitable example of others, the outside perspective on one's character offered by friends, and indeed, virtuous friendship is itself the communion and love which is presupposed by authentic Affective Maturity.

7. **Individual Formation Direction**: Individual guidance and attention is necessary for effective Human Formation. This has always been a part of the Christian Tradition, and is analogous to the role of the Spiritual Director, yet a distinct thing in and of itself and just as necessary.

8. **Individual Assessment**: Each individual person has been shaped in different ways by different experiences, and will grow and develop differently than others. It is vital

to have some form of ongoing assessment of individuals to facilitate positive Human Formation and healthy development.

9. **Personal Responsibility**: Any program of Human Formation will be ineffective unless the individual personally interiorizes the formation. Both the individual and those responsible for Human Formation are equally necessary cooperative causes in the individual's Human Formation.[33]

---

[33] See Mortimer J. Adler: "One man of virtue, thereby having practical knowledge [...] must be the efficient cause of the formation of virtue in another man, so that the latter gradually becomes able, through the practical knowledge which virtue gives, to regulate his own life. It remains true, of course, that the principle efficient cause of virtue must be a man's own acts, performed voluntarily and directed with prudence by his own reason. **The moral preceptor is, therefore, [...] a cooperative cause: moral training, like intellectual teaching, is an art of cooperating with nature, aiding the primary cause which is reason's own activity.** [...] The growing person may thus come to possess inchoate virtue before he knows the principles of moral theory and before he has practical knowledge whereby to regulate his own conduct. [...] By this route, it is possible for a man to become virtuous without ever being learned in moral theory. No one ever *becomes* virtuous simply by learning moral theory..." (*A Dialectic of Morals: Towards the Foundations of Political Philosophy*. New York: F. Ungar, 1958, p. 105-106).

10. **Humility:** Humility is the virtue that allows the heart to be moved in its desire to grow. It is, as it were, the "gateway" of virtue. Humility is not the same as self-deprecation. *Humility means the habit of* **knowing and embodying the truth about one's real self** *in relation to God, other persons, and the whole created order.* Humility is the virtue that prepares the fertile ground of the heart for communion. Before any intentional Human Formation can take place, the individual must have at least this basic level of humility: (a) the capacity for wonder and awe, (b) recognition of their basic weaknesses, and (c) the positive desire to become better.

Formative Experiences

The language of *Formative Experience* is the way to speak about the actual process by which Human Formation takes place. The Formative Experiences are divided into three basic kinds: **Aesthetic**, **Logical**, and **Relational**. To use the metaphor of sculpture, the Formative Experiences that shape the human person can be brief and momentary, like a chisel blow, or they can be slow and gradual, like a grinder or polishing brush.

Aesthetic: Aesthetic Formative Experience refers to the impact of the sensory environment (e.g. art, architecture, music, clothing, use of space). This is the most subtle but also most constant and accessible kind of Formative Experience. It engages the person directly on a pre-cognitive level.

Logical: Logical Formative Experience refers to the impact of rules, customs, and ethical-moral propositions of behavior (e.g. etiquette, law, proverbs). This kind of Formative Experience corresponds to the faculty of Reason and Cognition. This is the easiest of the three to attempt, and often the most focused on, but is also the least impactful if it lacks coherence with the other two kinds of Formative Experience. For instance, if the Logical Formative Experience of an individual is at cross-purposes to Aesthetic or Relational Formative Experience, the attempted Logical Formative Experience (e.g. rules & regulations) will at best be ineffective, and possibly even result in cynicism and duplicity.

Relational: Relational Formative Experience refers to the impact of personal encounters – human & divine (e.g. acquired mannerisms consciously or unconsciously picked up from others – accent, vocabulary, dress, attitude). This kind of Formative Experience has the deepest impact, and corresponds to the heart, the center of personhood, in relation to another person. Relational Formative Experience refers to anything from behaviors acquired through mimesis, to the deeper, less articulable impact of the intersubjective encounter between "I" and "Thou." It is the Relational Formative Experience, through the experience of intersubjectivity, that is the primary medium of Existential Affirmation or Validation of the Self.

Three Core Arenas

These Formative Experiences do not happen in a vacuum, but in real space and time; one has to take into account the spaces and roles that an individual occupies in daily life. These "spaces" are concretely lived-out relationship structures are referred to as the **"Three Core Arenas of Human Formation."**

To once again use the metaphor of sculpture: if the Formative Experiences are like the chisel-blows or polish-strokes on the marble block, then the very spaces that the marble takes up within the sculptor's studio are the Three Core Arenas. Although there are many roles, both formal and informal, that one occupies in life, the over-arching Arenas that are present in every person's life are the **Individual Arena**, the **Fraternal Arena**, and the **Institutional Arena**.

The Institutional Arena is that space where one interacts and relates as a member of a larger group or body. One relates as a part of a whole, which whole is distinct from its members. *Nota bene*: over-emphasis on this arena fosters an imbalanced immanent dimension of Self-Identity.

The Fraternal Arena is that space where one interacts and relates with others on a *personal* or *professional* peerage basis. One relates as a member of a smaller group of equals, which group is coterminous with its members. *Nota bene*: This arena ought to emphasize the balanced co-operation of persons in communion with one another.

The Individual Arena is that space where one acts in solitude or is addressed as an individual as the primary subject. *Nota bene*: over-emphasis on this arena fosters an imbalanced transcendent dimension of Self-Identity.

Tools of Human Formation

A "Tool of Human Formation" is an intentional process or structure within one or more of the Three Core Arenas, meant to encourage one or more Formative Experiences, essentially by creating the best possible environment for bringing about beneficial Formative Experiences. There are many tools for doing Human Formation, many ways it can be accomplished, which depend on multiple factors that vary greatly between organizations of different kinds (e.g. seminary, college, or a business corporation) and local circumstances. Some of the universally essential tools will be discussed in **Part III**.

Part III: Essential Practices for Human Formation in Action

Although the Tools for Human Formation will vary from organization to organization based on local circumstances, culture, and the kind of organization in which Human Formation is taking place, there are a few key tools and practices essential for putting an effective program of Human Formation into action in any organizational context, from the seminary and the college to the workplace and the home.

Verbal Instruction

As creatures endowed with intellect, we learn by instruction as well as by environment and example. The Word united within the Tradition is the very way that even the Church has been formed to seek to heal and perfect Human Nature. The goal of verbal instruction, both in written and oral form, is to articulate goals and the means of achieving them. Verbal Instruction can be seen often in the form of written rules or handbooks, but also includes such means as conferences, lectures, and even personal advice. Not all Verbal Instruction is as explicit as a rulebook or code of conduct. One of the most impactful forms of verbal instruction is through the media of books or films that inspire greatness of soul and provide exemplary models of character. Well-written biographies of great men and women can go a long way in shaping a person's character.

Community Structure

Any organization must have a stable and reliable structure of community if it is to help form Men and Women of Communion and Integrity. This applies to the entire community organization and hierarchy at all levels, which must provide a framework of stability within which individuals are free to mature and perfect their human qualities, and foster a virtuous formative environment. One of the vital characteristics of this is having a clear and reliable chain of command, avoiding conflicts of authority, and greater efficacy in resolving conflicts. It is also of supreme importance to designate leadership within the organization by merit-based promotion, and follow the principle of subsidiarity within the organization's essential hierarchy.

Small Fraternities

These are clearly defined subsidiary groups of individuals that ought to participate in regular common activity together in a formal and informal way.[34] The members of this fraternity should also meet on a weekly basis for peer consultation to mutually encourage one another in their own formation. This should happen through fraternal advice, fraternal correction, and mutual assistance. Such an arrangement provides a forum for consulting with one's peers about situations and relationships in a constructive and directed way.

Personal Formation Advisor

The process of Human Formation requires the individual direction of a prudent guide. This is embodied in the role of the Personal Formation Advisor, which is essential in any explicit program of Human Formation. This is a

---

[34] Particularly formative is the practice of eating meals together on a regular basis. Where closeness of living situation allows, it is preferable to have at least three meals per week in common.

mentor who personally accompanies and guides the individual's process of Human Formation. The goal of a Personal Formation Advisor is to oversee the individual's Human Formation, bringing him or her to authentic and mature Christian manhood or womanhood. The Personal Formation Advisor needs to foster a deep and authentic relationship of affective trust in order to effectively bring the individual to Affective Maturity. This requires vulnerability and transparency from both parties.

In order to ensure a healthy and beneficial development of an individual's Human Formation, the Personal Formation Advisor should be a trained and knowledgeable expert in Integrated Human Formation. He or she must be able to build a deep rapport with the individuals under his or her guidance, through vulnerability, love, and demonstrated loyalty.

Duties

The incorporation into a Human Formation program of specific "in-house" tasks for which the individual alone is responsible goes a long way in interiorizing one's personal responsibility to others and also forms reliability and diligence. These duties should rotate semi-regularly between individuals, and as the individual progresses in his or her Human Formation, these duties should become more complex and important.[35]

Personalized Plan

This is an individual's particular schedule and basic rules, drawn up under the guidance of his or her Personal Formation Advisor, that articulates general principles of Human Formation as they apply to the specific needs of the individual and exigencies of his or her personal circumstances and temperament.

Physical Activity

Regular activity that engages the totality of one's physical body, with at least moderate strain and exertion, has been shown to greatly improve a person's temperament and capacity

---

[35] *Nota bene*: Individuals should only be given greater responsibilities once they have demonstrated faithfulness in lesser duties.

for character formation. Human persons are embodied beings, and are made for physicality. It is a commonplace of ancient practical wisdom that physical activity combats the pathology of acedia, which is one of the besetting vices of Modern Western Society. Empirical evidence also has shown that regular physical activity improves confidence, mood, quality of sleep, and helps overcome depression and anxiety. Physical activity strengthens the integration of the person's Self-Identity and overall character.

Part IV. The Meta-Skills of Human Formation

The Meta-Skills

In the Cultivation of Virtue and the Acquisition of Practical Skills, and their reflexive Formation of the Heart – in short, the process of Human Formation in Action – there arises another vital dimension to becoming a Man or Woman of Communion. The three essential Meta-Skills of Human Formation stand out as unique in the process of growing in Affective Maturity; they don't just relate to specific virtues or skills, but to the very way that Virtues and the Formation of the Heart work.

These three Meta-Skills have a unique position vis-à-vis Affective Maturity, and through Affective Maturity, have their apex in the higher supernatural order. The Essential Part of Affective Maturity as precondition for self-mastery is **Mindfulness/Recollection**, Affective Maturity manifests itself in **Intuition into the Heart**, and the Man or Woman of Communion carries out his or her mission in the world through **Perfect Leadership**. The Meta-Skills are both interdependent and interpenetrating. They constitute both the very *essence* and *foundation* of the virtues, and are the *summative qualitative perfections* of all other virtues and skills. If a person had these Meta-Skills *perfectly*, one would be a Man or Woman of Communion in fact. Like any *habitus* of human character, they are developed by degrees through concrete intentional practices.

Mindfulness/Recollection

Mindfulness/Recollection is the Meta-Skill of being fully present in the task at hand and to the person before you. It is essentially **Full Self-Awareness** in relation to external reality, **Freedom** *from* **Distractedness**, and so **Freedom** *for* **Self-Possession**. The supernatural origin and end of Mindfulness/Recollection is the Interior Freedom of the children of God.[36] The fully recollected person is the most free person; authentic freedom means full presence and intentionality. As the Essential Part of the life of virtue, this Meta-Skill is what distinguishes

---

[36] Cf. "Creation itself will be set free from its bondage to decay and obtain the glorious *liberty of the children of God.*" Rom.8:21; and "For freedom Christ has set us free; stand fast therefore, and do not submit again to a yoke of slavery." Gal.5:1.

authentic virtue from mere simulacra, is the skill necessary in acquiring virtue, is the beginning of virtue as 'the examined life', and is the *telos* of virtue as 'natural contemplation'.

Intuition into the Heart

Intuition into the Heart is three-fold in nature: the skill of discerning and recognizing the emotional experience of another, based on verbal or behavioral cues; an empathic knowledge of the human condition and deepest longings of the human heart; and the loving disposition toward the other as beloved son or daughter of our Father in Heaven. Intuition into the Human Heart is the natural foundation oriented to the Beatific Vision. The greatest Human Heart to have insight into is the Heart of Christ, "who knew what was in humanity."[37]

Intuition into the Human Heart is the most difficult Meta-Skill to form, since its primary component is Wisdom, which comes from on high. This is not to say that this component of

---

[37] John 2:25

Human Formation requires the intervention of the supernatural as such, but that the role of natural formation in this regard is to form the appetite to orient to wisdom so that wisdom might be desired and sought (*philo-sophia*), and to remove the typical impediments[38] to wisdom in the life of the individual person.

Perfect Leadership

Rooted in the Cardinal Virtues, the Meta-Skill of Leadership leads the individual beyond himself or herself, with a magnanimity informed by the human perfection which shines forth in Christ. Perfect Leadership orients man beyond himself, beyond human nature, and finds its supernatural origin and end in the individual's participation in the Divine Mission of the Church, whether that is carried out as an international figurehead, the director of a school, or as a parent. The Meta-Skill of Perfect Leadership is the multiplying of one's own virtues into others, leading them into virtue, and deepening the virtues in their

---

[38] i.e. egocentrism, habitual sin, distractedness, & materialism.

own character.   Perfect Leadership means leading others into perfection, into the good life, in all aspects.

Natural Orientation to a Supernatural End

These Meta-Skills are, within the scope of Human Formation, the natural foundation and orientation to its supernatural end, for to be truly and most perfectly a Man or Woman of Communion – the very goal of Human Formation – necessarily entails the perfection of supernatural Charity, which is the "form of the virtues" in the divinized life of Grace. The Man or Woman of Communion in the natural order finds his or her completion in a supernatural end: Communion with God in Christ, who is Himself *the* Man of Communion.

Suggested Practices for the Meta-Skills

As mentioned above, these Meta-Skills are acquired, like any *habitus* of human character, by degrees and through concrete practices. While the Meta-Skills are built up through the practice of the Virtues and Practical Skills, there are some specific exercises and principles that can be applied to developing each of the Meta-Skills in a direct way as well.

Practical Exercises for Mindfulness

The habit of Mindfulness/Recollection can be cultivated through small but significant practical exercises done each day to strengthen your attention and awareness of what is happening in the world around you as well as the movements of your own heart. Taking a small amount of time each day for brief exercises like these will help you develop a more continuous awareness of your thoughts, your feelings, and the world around you. By their very nature, these exercises will also become a means for reducing stress and distractedness in your life.

Practical Exercise 1: Becoming Aware of the World Around You

1. Periodically throughout the day, take a brief moment to pay particular attention to what you see around you. Notice the colors, movement, vibrancy, and details of at least five different objects in your environment.

2. A few times a day, take a few moments to become aware of what you hear. So often we tune out anything not particularly relevant to our immediate task, so it is easy to miss important and often beautiful things. Notice the sounds around you, try to distinguish them from one another, become aware of the volume, timbre, and pitch of each sound.

3. At least once each day, take some time to become aware of the aromas and scents that you smell. Notice your reaction to various scents, and try to recognize what the particular quality of each scent is.

4. During some task that you are working on, bring your attention to the feel of whatever you are touching, whether a tool, a computer, pencil, clothing, or whatever. Notice whether it is hard or soft, hot or cold, rough or smooth.

5. Eat at least one meal each day at a slower pace, intentionally savoring the flavor of your food and drink. Become aware of the complexity of flavor and aroma, the feel of it on your tongue and the full sensory experience of eating.

Practical Exercise 2: Becoming Aware of Your Thoughts & Emotions

1. Take 2-3 minutes each morning and evening to relax, leave what you're doing, take a few deep breaths, and become of what you are thinking and feeling. Notice any places of tension that you might be holding in your muscles, and take a moment to release that tension. As you do this, you may notice various thoughts arising or emotions that you are feeling. Learn to recognize the origin and development of these thoughts and emotions, and realize that you are not identical to your thoughts and feelings.

Often we pay no attention to our thoughts or feelings, but let them take total control over us before we even notice that they are there. In order to attain greater self-possession and peace of soul, we need to learn to become aware of our thoughts and emotions as they are just beginning to arise, and learn to distinguish what thoughts and emotions we want to embrace, and those we want to let go.

2. Take a moment or two throughout the day to pause what you're doing and become aware of what you are thinking and feeling. This is a good periodic exercise to develop the ability to recognize thoughts and feelings before they take total hold of your heart. Recognize the thoughts or emotions as distinct from who you are, and see them as objects floating on a stream in your mind. You are free to embrace them or let them pass. Take a moment to see where this or that particular thought or emotion is coming from. Get to the point where you are able to decide which thoughts and emotions you will allow to access your heart and which you will discard. This will be difficult at first, but with practice and time you will become able to do it without much effort.

Guidelines for Developing Intuition into the Heart

In order to develop the Meta-Skill of Intuition into the Heart, you need to work on removing the impediments to wisdom such as distractedness and egocentrism from your life, and also work on cultivating the desire for wisdom. Another important thing to do, which helps with the first two tasks, is to cultivate stillness in your life. Learn to see yourself as you truly are. Learn to see others as real selves, and understand them in our shared human condition.

Practices to Remove Impediments to Wisdom

1. Overcome egocentrism (being self-absorbed, looking out primarily for your own interests) by noticing opportunities to give of yourself in small ways for the good of others. This can be something as simple getting into the habit of holding doors for others, or even helping another with their study, work, or chores. Learn to look out for the needs of others.

2. The practice of regular and moderate fasting can go a long way in overcoming materialism. By giving up small things (e.g. extra portions, certain extra flavoring, digital technology) from time to time, you learn to seek what is higher than material needs and comfort.

3. Get into the habit of regularly silencing your cell-phone and other mobile devices. Overcome the need to check them constantly. Learn to moderate your use of mobile devices or computers. One very helpful practice to cut down on distraction in your life is to limit yourself to checking email only in the late morning (after some work is done) and late afternoon.

4. Develop the habit of keeping to one physical task for an extended period of time without distraction.

Practices to Cultivate the Desire for Wisdom

1. Take up the practice of keeping a journal of your thoughts and emotions each day. Becoming aware of your own thoughts and emotions, and how quickly they pass and change can help you realize the fleeting nature of things that may seem immense in the moment they are experienced. Honestly acknowledging your weaknesses and shortcomings can also help you understand and sympathize with the shortcomings of other people as well.

2. Take some time to regularly examine your own life: where you have been, what you are doing now, and where you may go in life. Then consider the life of someone much older than yourself: what they might have been like when they were very young, what they may have been doing when they were your age, and what they are like now. Then consider a very young child: what this child's life might be like, what this child might be like when he or she is your age, and when he or she becomes aged and elderly. Recognize that you too were once that age, and that you are aging every day. Consider what kind of life you want to live, and realize that the paths of all people begin and end the same: we are born, and we die, and what each person, young or old, has at any moment in their possession is the same – him or herself in the present moment.

3. Occasionally call to mind the fact that you will at some point leave this life, and you do not know when. Live so that whenever that moment might come, your life will be a well-lived one. This should bring into perspective any worries and troubles you may have in life.

4. Regularly get away from city life to spend some time in the wilderness and look up at the night sky. Behold the stars and gaze at them in wonder and awe.

Practices to Cultivate Stillness and Insight

1. Like the exercise listed above for cultivating Mindfulness, take a few minutes at the beginning and end of each day to relax, be still, and calm your thoughts.

2. As you begin to develop the ability to notice your thoughts and emotions as they come and go throughout the day, start to pay attention to what causes them and what your reaction is to various thoughts and feelings. Recognize that other people have the same experiences and reactions just as you do, to different things perhaps, but that they are not so different from you nor you from them. Begin to understand them as other selves.

3. Get into the practice of taking a "technology Sabbath" or "technology fast": spend a whole day without using mobile devices or computers. A good way to ease into this is to spend some time every day away from these devices or having them turned off at certain times during the day.

4. Spend time outside, in the wilderness or a garden if possible, and just sit in the stillness and tranquility that you find there. Let the concerns and thoughts of the day leave you behind, and just watch the natural world progressing at its own pace around you.

5. Go into some crowded place and step aside from the crowd. Watch the people as they pass by, look at their faces, notice their expressions and the small gestures of their hands, notice their body language as they encounter one another. Try to recognize what some of these expressions and gestures might mean, what it shows about that person's thoughts, feelings, and desires. Learn to see them as your brothers and sisters.

Principles for Forming Leaders

In order to learn the art of leadership, one needs to gain experience leading. This seems simple enough, but what is often overlooked is the importance of becoming a *good* leader (not just one who is good at leading) by first learning to follow the leadership of others. In order to advance to greater responsibilities, a person needs to demonstrate that he or she is faithful and competent in lesser responsibilities. This is what it means for leadership to be acquired by degrees.

Even prior to gaining experience in leading, the first thing that must be done is to instill a solid dedication to the mission.[39] It is not enough to desire to lead out of a lust for power; the individual must be motivated in his or her leadership out of sincere dedication to the cause, whatever it may be. Even the leader who is the head of his or her organization must subordinate himself or herself to the mission, the purpose for which he or she is leading, which is higher than the leaders themselves. This dedication can be instilled

---

[39] Cf. *Dedication & Leadership,* by Douglas Hyde. Published by University of Notre Dame Press, 1966.

in many ways, but however it is instilled and whatever the cause, true leadership will be most effective when it is united to sincere dedication.

In order to form leaders, it is necessary to place individuals in actual situations of leadership as soon as and as often as possible. It need not be a vital task – you should never delegate an unproven leader to a critical task – but it should be one that challenges the delegated individual to grow beyond their current competency. Although it may seem that the future leader should be equipped with as many skills as possible prior to taking on any leadership responsibility, it is precisely in taking on some level of authority that the individual recognizes and appreciates their need, and so acquires these skills more thoroughly and efficiently than they would otherwise.

The following are some basic principles that should guide how you form men and women for leadership[40]:

1. You should delegate the individual to lead specific tasks from time to time, under your supervision (not under your micromanagement), that are above and beyond the normal scope of his or her duties.

2. Immediately after the task is accomplished, you should take *two minutes* alone with the delegated leader and critique his or her choices and directives in an up-front and honest way, being harsh, but fair.

3. After that, take *five minutes* with the whole group and point out his or her successes.

Notice the way in which steps two and three are carried out: Chastise in private, praise in public. Spend more time in affirmation than in criticism.

---

[40] I am grateful to my good friend, Capt Lucas H. Forcella of the United States Marine Corps, for recommending these principles to me.

Part V. A Guide to the Virtues

Two Complementary Approaches to the Virtues

A comprehensive and systematic understanding of Human Formation must approach the virtues from two complementary perspectives, the **Programmatic** and the **Ontological**. *The Programmatic approach* organizes the virtues according to practical acquisition. The Programmatic approach is the developmental way to speak about the virtues, and addresses how the virtues are related to one another within various actions and circumstances. The Programmatic approach organizes the virtues according to their interdependency in a programmatic or developmental hierarchy. It is the more complex of the two perspectives. *The Ontological approach* organizes the virtues according to their ontological taxonomy, that is, it organizes the virtues according to their specific origin within the person, their ends, and their object. The Ontological approach provides a systematic taxonomy of the virtues as they exist in relation to one another on an abstracted, scientific level. It provides the definitive organization of the virtues according to *genus* and *species*.

In order to proceed with a successful Programmatic approach to the virtues, you first need to have a vision of the definitional principles provided by the Ontological approach. The following charts and descriptions provide a comprehensive overview of the virtues according to their Ontological organization – according to the principles regarding their acts, origins, and ends. The actual development of virtue is much more complex and interweaving than a systematic taxonomy, but such a taxonomy is necessary for understanding the nature of the virtues in themselves, which in turn is required before being able to understand the Programmatic relationships among the virtues.

The Continuum of Character Traits

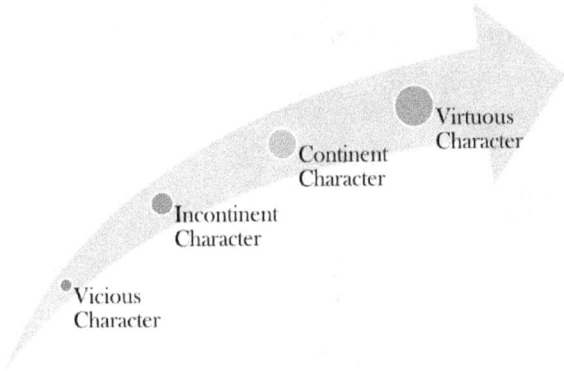

Virtue, as mentioned above, is a habit of character that is acquired by degrees and over time. Just like acquiring any skill, the process of acquiring virtue means a person's character may fall anywhere along a continuous spectrum of character traits in regard to a particular virtue. This continuum of virtue acquisition shows the spectrum of degrees to which a particular virtue is possessed, from not having the virtue at all (completely vicious) to complete mastery of the virtue (completely virtuous).

Continuum of Character Traits

Virtuous
Character

Continent
Character

Incontinent
Character

Vicious
Character

These Character Traits are defined as follows:

Vicious Character: "Unconsciously Unskilled" in regard to a particular virtue; this person neither recognizes nor does the right thing in the right way at the right time, but rather takes pleasure in actions that are harmful.

Incontinent Character: "Consciously Unskilled" in regard to a particular virtue; this person desires to do the right thing, but fails to do so either out of weakness or out of ignorance.

Continent Character: "Consciously Skilled" in regard to a particular virtue; this person both knows and does the right thing, but only through sheer effort and force of will. He or she finds the idea of virtue attractive, but takes no pleasure in the right action in and of itself.

Virtuous Character: "Unconsciously Skilled" in regard to a particular virtue; this person knows and does the right thing as though it were second nature, without much conscious effort or exertion. He or she takes pleasure in the right action in and of itself.

The Cardinal Virtues

The moral virtues are generally categorized according to two levels: the Cardinal Virtues and the Subsidiary Virtues. The Cardinal Virtues are the four primary and foundational virtues of which every other virtue (of the Subsidiary Virtues) is a species. The four Cardinal Virtues are Prudence, Justice, Fortitude, and Temperance. Each of the Cardinal Virtues will be described below, along with their respective Subsidiary Virtues.

The Four Cardinal Virtues

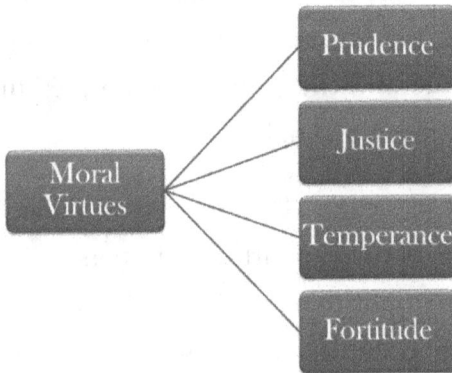

Prudence and its Subsidiary Virtues

Prudence is the strength of character that is the habit of deliberating well and putting right decision into action in the right way and at the right time. In other words, it is the habit of knowing what to do in appropriate circumstances, *and* actually following through by doing it. Prudence is generally opposed to Imprudence (deciding on and doing the wrong thing), Negligence, Guile (deception or duplicity), and Indecision and Unreliability.

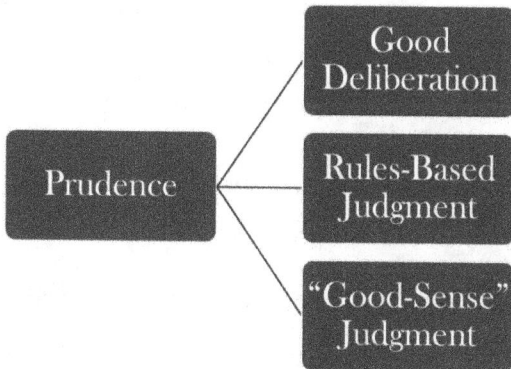

The Subsidiary Virtues of Prudence are as follows:

Good Deliberation: This is the habit of thoughtfulness or deliberating well, taking good counsel and planning things out accordingly.

Rules-Based Judgment: This is the habit of sound practical judgment of general cases, pertaining to the law and prescriptive rules.

"Good Sense" Judgment: This is the habit of sound practical judgment in exceptional cases where prescriptive law no longer is appropriate, pertaining to the greater good according to the universal law of nature.

Prudence itself is specified according to five different domains requiring its exercise:

Individual Prudence: deciding well and acting rightly in regard to one's own relation to the good.

Governmental Prudence: good and effective leadership of others in an organization.

Civic Prudence: deciding well and acting rightly in regard to the common good, the law, and one's responsibility to others – reliability.

Domestic Prudence: the ability to effectively and rightly manage one's family, financial, and domestic concerns and responsibilities.

Military Prudence: deciding well and acting rightly in military or strategic affairs.

Justice and its Subsidiary Virtues

Justice is that strength of character that is the habit of healthy and respectful relationships with others, marked by honesty and integrity. Justice is the virtue that allows a person to relate and interact well with other persons, society as a whole, and God.

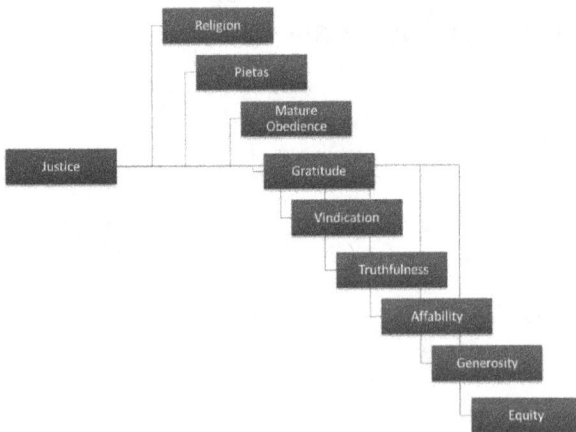

The Subsidiary Virtues of Justice are as follows:

Religion: This is the habit of cultivating a healthy and reverent relationship with God and all things sacred. This means offering to God what is due to Him as creator of all things, and upright action and attitude toward matters of worship, ritual, and prayer. It also is the strength of being devoted to God in a relationship of loyalty. This virtue is the opposite of the vices of superstition, idolatry, sacrilege, perjury, and false worship. It is important to note that the virtue of Religion is a *natural virtue (i.e. rooted in our own human nature)*, and not to be confused with the supernatural or theological virtue of faith. The realm of the theological virtues, and of spirituality in general, depends upon this natural foundation in the natural moral virtue of Religion. Without this natural virtue, one tends toward a superstitious and psychologically unhealthy approach to spirituality.

Pietas: This is the habit of reverence, respect, and honor given to one's family, ancestors, and relatives. It also includes cultivating a healthy honor and affection for one's home and compatriots. It is opposed to the vices of nationalism/partisanship and betrayal, as well as the vice of enmeshment in family relationships.

Mature Obedience: This is the habit of reverence, respect, and honor for persons in a position of dignity and authority. It is opposed to both the vice of disobedience and the vice of unquestioning submission.

Gratitude: This is the habit of humble recognition of services and gifts provided by others. It is the habit of cultivating thanks in all appropriate circumstances and manifesting appropriate gratitude toward one's benefactors. It is opposed to both ingratitude and insecure appeasement.

Vindication: The habit of lawfully seeking justice when one has been wronged. This justice is motivated by charity, rather than by wrath. It is opposed to the vices of vengefulness and that vice which allows oneself to be abused and trampled on by others.

Truthfulness: This is the habit of honesty and transparency in one's relationships with others. It is opposed to the vices of lying, hypocrisy, bragging, and false humility.

Affability: This is the habit of friendliness, kindliness, and being an enjoyable person to be around. It is opposed to both flattery and quarrelsomeness.

Generosity: This is the habit of sharing one's goods with others for their own sake. This virtue is opposed to both covetousness and the wasteful or reckless doling out of one's own resources.

Equity: This is the habit of right judgment and action toward others in dispensing with legislative prescriptions when in particular circumstances a technical application of the law would be in fact unjust. It is the virtue of supra-legal justice for others.

Fortitude and its Subsidiary Virtues

Fortitude is that character strength which is the habit of steadfast courage in facing challenges and difficulties. This virtue is the balance of strength that overcomes the weakness of needless fear, rashness, and brazen fearlessness. Fortitude is the strength to implement decisions you've made, do great things in spite of difficulty, and persevere under pressure, and resiliency in overcoming obstacles and hardship.

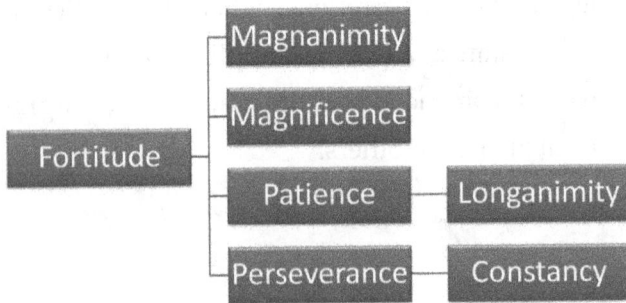

The Subsidiary Virtues of Fortitude are as follows:

Magnanimity: This is the habit of striving for greatness. The word itself means 'great-souled-ness'. It is the strength to pursue and undertake great and noble endeavors, inspired by the hope of attaining something difficult to reach. It is the strength which overcomes presumption and pusillanimity (small-souledness). While the pusillanimous person shrinks from striving after great things and prefers the comfort of mediocrity and normalcy, the magnanimous person boldly takes the initiative to lead – alone, if necessary – the undertaking to fulfill his or her God-given mission for greatness.

Magnificence: This is the habit of greatness in one's works on behalf of others. It is the virtue of generosity in regard to great things which must be done and require great expense of one's own resources. It is the strength which overcomes meanness and the fear of material loss.

Patience: This is the habit of calmly facing with balanced-mind and tranquility the sufferings imposed by others. This is also known as 'Resiliency' or 'Hardiness'. It is the strength which overcomes fragility, unresponsiveness, and a temperamental attitude.

Longanimity: This sub-species of Patience is the habit of hopeful endurance for a delayed good. It is the habit of being able to wait for delayed gratification. It is the strength which overcomes discouragement and inconstancy.

Perseverance: This is the habit of persisting in the good, pushing back against the difficulty faced in the very continuance of whatever one is doing. It is the strength which overcomes laziness and softness as well as pertinacity.

Constancy: This sub-species of Perseverance is the habit of persevering in the good amidst obstacles encountered in addition to the difficulty inherent in the nature of prolonged action. It is the habit of sticking with something despite difficulty, and of quitting when the time is right. It is the strength which overcomes both resignation and stubbornness.

Temperance and its Subsidiary Virtues

Temperance is the strength of character that is the habit of rightly directing one's emotions, feelings, and desires. Temperance is the virtue that overcomes both over-indulgence and insensitivity. The one who is temperate is a man or woman who desires and enjoys the right kind of pleasures in the appropriate way and in the right amount. In other words, it is the habit of taking appropriate measure of things according to circumstance. This necessarily involves sincerity and integrity in one's behavior and actions.

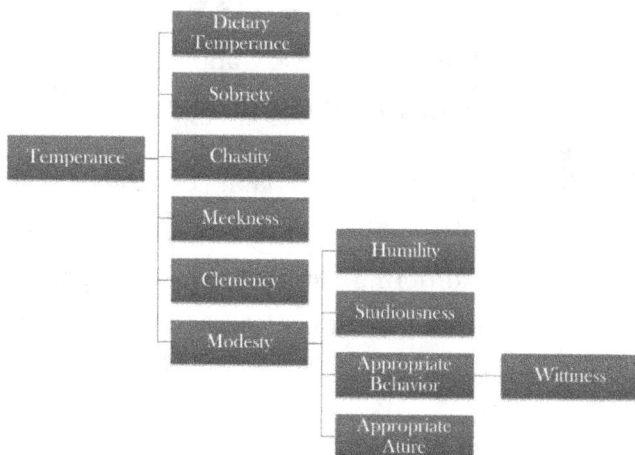

The Subsidiary Virtues of Temperance are as follows:

Dietary Temperance: This is the habit of right enjoyment of food. It is the habit of eating a healthy and balanced diet of nutritious food, in the proper quantity, and appropriate enjoyment of the taste and quality of one's food. It is the balance opposed to both insensitivity to good food and over-indulgence in terms of quantity or delicacy.

Sobriety: This is the habit of appropriate enjoyment of alcoholic beverages, the balance between total abstinence and drinking to get drunk. The same also applies to other substances such as caffeine and nicotine.

Chastity: This is the habit of appropriate ordering of sexual desire and feelings. It is the balanced ordering of desire that opposes repression and emotional frigidity as well as lust and seduction.

Meekness: This is the habit of appropriately directing one's emotional response in the face of offense or affliction. It is the proper balance of assertiveness and tranquility that opposes both inordinate anger and spinelessness.

Clemency: This is the habit of appropriate leniency towards others, especially subordinates. It is the right balance which opposes both cruelty and permissiveness.

Modesty: This is the habit of right ordering both one's own attentiveness and the desire for the attention of others. It deals largely with appropriateness regarding one's own self.

Humility: This is the habit of knowing and becoming who you really are. True humility is the authenticity to recognize your dependence on God and that he has made you for great and noble things. In a word, true humility is authenticity. It is opposed to both narcissism and pride on the one hand, and self-degradation on the other.

Studiousness: This is the habit of keeping one's attention focused on important things and open to a spirit of wonder and awe. It is the appropriate directing of the mind which opposes ignorance and superficiality as well as the gluttonous consumption of information.

Appropriate Behavior: This is the habit of behaving appropriately in varying circumstances, opposed to excessive formality or finicky behavior on the one hand, and unprofessionalism or immaturity on the other.

Wittiness: This is the habit of making enjoyable conversation through the clever presentation of the irony in life. Wittiness is the skill of speaking appropriately to the circumstances, and is opposed to both excessive or uncouth joking and somber lack of humor.

Appropriate Attire: This is the habit of dressing appropriately to the circumstances: formality in formal situations and casual attire in informal situations. In other words, it is the habit of dressing for the occasion – whether work, play, dance, or dinner. It entails paying enough attention to maintaining one's appearance, without vanity or preening.

Part VI. A Guide to the Practical Skills

Personal Skills & Social Skills

As mentioned above,[41] the Practical Skills facilitate the Gift of Self in the real, concrete circumstances of everyday life. They also serve as concrete measurable indicators of virtuous habits. The Practical Skills listed below are organized into two general categories: *Personal* and *Social*, each of which is further divided into three specific categories according to the object of each skill. These skills are interrelated and mutually dependent in many cases. The list is not exhaustive, but gives a sense of the general nature and place that the Practical Skills have within the Art & Science of Human Formation.

---

[41] **Part I: Acquisition of Practical Skills**

Practical Skills I: The Personal Skills

Religious	Physical	Psychological
Discipline of Prayer	Exercise	Stress Management
Diligence in Sacramental Practice	Sleep	Leisure
Regular Examination of Conscience	Diet	Time Management
Meditative Reading	Hygiene	Mindfulness
Silence		Self Discipline with Technology
Simplicity of Life		Emotional Self-Regulation

Religious Practice

The Discipline of Prayer: The discipline of regularly making time for explicit prayer throughout the daily, weekly, and annual cycles of life. Includes an appropriate balance of public liturgical prayer and private personal prayer

Diligence in Sacramental Practice: Regular and sincere participation in the Sacraments of the Church. Entails understanding the nature of the Sacraments and appreciation for their place in the life of the Christian

Regular Examination of Conscience: Taking time on a regular basis for a structured and thorough examination of one's moral state and assess the progress in specific virtues or skills and presence of particular areas for growth

Meditative Reading: Readily makes time for thoughtful and immersive reading of writings that edify and elevate one's aspirations

Silence: Cultivating both an exterior and interior demeanor of silence; healthy comfort with silence and solitude

Simplicity of Life: Maintaining a balanced and integrated lifestyle and a prudent but dedicated involvement in a limited amount of activities

Physical Self-Care

Exercise: Regular, vigorous, and disciplined exercise that challenges strength and endurance in order to maintain and continuously improve fitness of both mind and body

Sleep: Discipline in keeping to set times for going to bed and waking up that allows for optimal sleep according to individual needs (typically between 7-8 hours/night), and making use of brief naps during the day

Diet: Maintaining healthy eating habits both in terms of quantity, moderate pace of eating, regular frequency, and nutritional content according to individual needs

Hygiene: Keeping clean and trimmed (hair & nails), washing hands before eating, attending to grooming and cleanliness needs on a regular basis and keeping up with regular physical and dental check-ups. Also requires maintaining clean and sanitary environment (room, office, bathroom)

Psychological Self-Care

Stress Management: Healthy response to stress and able to accomplish effective stress-reduction, as well as ability to manage priorities and urgent tasks in efficient and timely manner and avoiding distress in the first place

Leisure: The ability to make space and time amidst the cycle of work and recovery for relaxing, refreshing, and creative life-giving activities.

Time Management: Ability to manage one's work and responsibilities with realistic amounts of time dedicated to necessary tasks, and the discipline of maintaining focus on important tasks for extended periods of time.

Mindfulness: This is the Practical Skill component of the Meta-Skill mentioned above in Part IV, and consists in the discipline of maintaining awareness of objects and movement in one's immediate environment and interior movements of the heart.

Self-Discipline with Technology: Moderate use of screen-technology and ability to maintain healthy human interaction in the physical world

Emotional Self-Regulation: Awareness of one's own emotional states and reactions, and ability to feel and express emotions appropriately and in a healthy way

Practical Skills II: The Social Skills

Relationship	Deportment	Professional
Boundaries	Social Etiquette	Leadership
Response to Emotional Cues	Conversation	Public Speaking
Conflict Management	Dress	Management/Teamwork
Recreation	Posture	Negotiation
Disciplined use of Social Media & Mass Communication	Eloquence	Financial Management

Relationship

Boundaries: Observes appropriate boundaries both physical and emotional/conversational with men and women

Response to Emotional Cues: Effective and appropriate response to the emotional cues of others

Conflict Management: Effective de-escalation of conflict situations while retaining self-possession

Recreation: Appropriate means of social recreation, as well as skill in many forms of recreation (e.g. sports, cards)

Disciplined Use of Social Media & Mass Communication: Disciplined and appropriate use of Social Media & observing appropriate self-disclosure boundaries with Mass Communication Media

Deportment

Social Etiquette: Appropriate forms of address and public behavior, phone call response times, thank you cards, guidelines for tipping, etc.

Conversation: Ability to comfortably converse with others, free from awkwardness and anxiety, while maintaining appropriate levels of self-disclosure

Dress: Well-dressed and clothed appropriately for the situation (from formalwear to farm-work, liturgy to landscaping)

Posture: Healthy and confident poise that is neither pretentious nor slovenly

Eloquence: Speaking well in a persuasive manner both pleasing to the hearer and effective in conveying ones intention and ideas

Professional

Leadership: This is the Practical Skill component of the Meta-Skill mentioned above in Part IV, and is the ability to gain the respect of, motivate, organize, and direct others while bearing the weight of responsibility for the outcome

Public Speaking: Eloquence, ease, and effectiveness speaking to a crowd

Management: Working cooperatively with colleagues, and managing employees both individually and corporately

Negotiation: Effective in negotiating outcomes mutually beneficial to all involved; and having a good sense of what is negotiable and what is not

Financial Management: Basic money-managing know-how as an individual and as a man or woman responsible for the material needs of others

A Final Note

To those responsible for the Human Formation of others:

Human Formation is an urgent and important work of Divine Charity. Any program of Human Formation is carrying out its work *in persona Christi Formator* – Christ the Perfect Formator of Human Nature. Those responsible for Human Formation must always bear in mind that they too are in need of ongoing and continual formation themselves. They are responsible for the formation they impart on two levels: that of their words and that of their deeds, their own character. Those responsible for the Human Formation of others must therefore be solicitous for the welfare of those under their guidance, and work continuously that while they are forming others, they themselves should grow in Affective Maturity.[42] We are not perfect yet, but should be undergoing continually the formation of our own natural human qualities to the perfection which shines forth in the Incarnate Son of God.

---

[42] Cf. *Rule of St. Benedict*, 2.

"Not that I have already obtained this or am already perfect; but I press on to make it my own, because Christ Jesus has made me his own."[43]

[43] Philippians 3:12

Appendix: Sample Outline of Human Formation Plan for Individual Use

An example of how some of the principles, practices, and tools outlined above might be put into practice in a basic and simple way.

1. Personal Plan: a schema for one's daily life, containing at least the following elements

- Routine for Physical Activity: one hour of physical exercise every day

- A Plan for good sleeping habits:

    o In bed by 10pm, wake up with alarm at 6am

    o Wind down before bedtime with relaxing activity

- A Plan for healthy eating habits:

    o Balanced diet

    o Consistent meal schedule

    o Eating with attentiveness to one's food/not rushing gluttonously through it

- Hygiene: foster the discipline of regular cleanliness and grooming habits

- Cultivating the Habit of Mindfulness/Recollection: ½ hour of concrete mindfulness practices each day

- A Plan for regular religious practices

2. Daily and Weekly Self-Examination of one's character and development

3. Regularly Read Good Biographies of great men & women, exemplars of magnanimity. Consider how to imitate their spirit and character.

4. Attend Monthly Conferences on Human Formation topics

5. Personal Formation Advisor: Meet weekly for ongoing individual direction

6. Small Fraternity:

- Meet weekly for "peer consultations"

- Discuss virtuous living

- Regular common activities (sports, outings, etc.)

- Frequent shared meals in common

7. Leadership: focus on person-centered (leading with character) for those leadership roles one has in life

Nota Bene: Not all of the items on this list are of equal weight; numbers **(2)**, **(5)**, and **(6)** are the key drivers of Human Formation, which contribute over 75% of the progress of Human Formation, supported by the other items on the list. All the points on the list are equally essential, but these three (**2**, **5**, & **6**) are the dynamo of the system in this particular example.

About the Author

Cameron M. Thompson is a researcher and educator specializing in Philosophy of the Human Person and Moral Psychology. He received his Master of Arts degree in Catholic Studies from the University of St. Thomas in St. Paul, MN. He regularly teaches both high school and college courses, and is co-founder and director of Acropolis Scholars, LLC, a cultural and educational company. Cameron is available for consultation on Human Formation with organizations, schools, and with individuals.

For more information on Human Formation, or to arrange a speaking engagement or consulting appointment, you may contact him at HumanFormation@acropolisscholars.com.

www.ingramcontent.com/pod-product-compliance
Lightning Source LLC
Chambersburg PA
CBHW052055270326
41931CB00012B/2767